Original title: Crafting the Inner Muse

Author: Daisy Dewi
Editor: Jessica Elisabeth Luik
ISBN 978-9916-39-519-6

Crafting the Inner Muse

Daisy Dewi

The Resonance of Concealed Beauty

Beneath the veils of worldly guise,
Lies grace that often goes unseen,
A splendor subtle to our eyes,
Within, it whispers, soft and keen.

In every soul there lives a glow,
A quiet beauty, pure and true,
Its light, through cracks, begins to show,
The more we seek, the more it grew.

This hidden charm in plainest things,
A melody that sweetly sings,
In whispers of the fluttering wings,
And in the peace that solace brings.

Concealed, yet felt in lovers' sighs,
In kindred spirits, it arises,
A resonance no mask can hide,
In every heart, it quietly presides.

Batons of the Invisible Orchestra

Silent batons rise and fall,
In the symphony of life's grand hall,
Conducting winds and strings unseen,
The music felt, where it has been.

Each wave, each pulse, a silent note,
Crafting an invisible coat,
Worn by the world in harmonized pride,
In this concert, we all coincide.

Nature’s maestro, deft and wise,
Commands the sun, the seas, the skies,
With every dawn, a fresh overture,
Life’s ensemble plays on, pure and sure.

In the dance of stars and cosmic grace,
There lies a rhythm in the silent space,
Batons of the invisible orchestra roam,
In the quiet universe, we call home.

The Harbinger of Creative Dawn

In twilight's cusp, ideas take flight,
A muse descends, shrouded in night,
The harbingers of dawn, they come,
With strokes of genius, deft and bright.

From slumbering minds, new thoughts arise,
As stars that twinkle in dark skies,
The silent seeds of day to sow,
Inventing worlds, where wonder lies.

In painted hues of morning's first glow,
Imagination starts to grow,
With each creation's hopeful yawn,
The birth of art, a sacred show.

So heed the call of untamed morn,
Embrace the quests you have not worn,
The herald of creative spawn,
An endless cycle, thus reborn.

The Sculptor's Breath

In marble halls where silence dwells,
He carves the winds, the stories tells.
With chisel's kiss, the stone imbued,
Life emerges, rough, subdued.

Veins of dust through fingers slide,
A sculptor's breath, the spark inside.
An ethereal dance, a timeless leap,
From within the block, dreams seep.

Cold figure warm with sculptor's love,
Capturing motion, dove above.
Art, the prisoner set free,
In the sculptors' breath, it's key.

Melodies Unseen

Whispers float on silent air,
Notes that paint the day so fair.
A symphony so sweet, confined,
In the quiet corners of the mind.

Waves unseen by naked eyes,
In the haunting silence lies.
Melodies that touch the heart,
Without a sound, they impart.

Strings that vibrate without touch,
Songs that move us, oh so much.
The music in a lover's sigh,
Melodies unseen, yet they fly.

Chasing the Artful Demons

Through the canvas maze, we run,
Seeking shadow, seeking sun.
Demons dance in splattered ink,
In this artful chaos, we sink.

Colors blend in wild pursuit,
Chasing dreams in each stroke's root.
Artful demons lead the chase,
In expressive lines, they grace.

Canvas snares the dauntless soul,
Hunting beauty is our role.
Across the void, brushstrokes sweep,
Demons chased, in art we leap.

The Quiet Storm of Ideas

In the mind's eye, a silent storm,
Ideas brew, take shape and form.
Underneath the placid sphere,
The tempest of thought draws near.

Ripples in the gray expanse,
Alive with the creative dance.
Quietly, the lightning arcs,
Igniting fires from stray sparks.

This storm of minds, rarely heard,
Whirling with potential, stirred.
A whisper of what could be,
In the storm, our ideas free.

The Inventor's Stillness

In the inventor's hush, gears cease their spin,
Tools lay at rest from the toils within.
Blueprints unfurl like scrolls of old,
Capturing dreams in their sketched-fold.

In solitude's embrace ideas take flight,
Each calculation cast in the pale moonlight.
A spark ignites in the stillness of mind,
As visions of cogs and pistons intertwined.

The quiet bears witness to creation's birth,
In the silence, solutions unearth.
From the tranquil night, day's labor born,
A world reshaped by the time of morn.

In amazement, the inventor stands still,
As new contraptions bend to will.
The workshop whispers with unseen hands,
In the inventor's stillness, progress expands.

The Ethereal Weaver

Softly threads the weaver of the night,
Weaving dreams with gossamer and light.
Each delicate strand glowing fair,
In the tapestry of the midnight air.

The loom of stars, her sacred grove,
She orchestrates the dance above.
The shuttle flies in her ghostly grip,
Crafting fantasies on celestial ship.

Silken patterns in the sky unfurl,
Each a dream cast from her world.
The weaver's touch, unseen but felt,
Where the fabric of night and wishes melt.

Her ethereal garment drapes the space,
A garment of the cosmos laced.
Invisible hands, her artistry's seal,
The weaver spins the universe’s wheel.

Plucking the Strings of Essence

Upon the strings of essence plucked,
The melody of the soul, not lucked.
Notes resonate from the heart's own tune,
Singing truths that swoon too soon.

Fingers dance on vibrational threads,
Awakening feelings that in shadows led.
Harmonies born from the innermost core,
Reverberating with the silence no more.

A symphony of being, raw and clear,
As the minstrel of existence draws near.
Strumming life's cadences, wild and free,
In the universal song, we find our key.

The chords connect in profound mime,
Echoing through the corridors of time.
Each life, a note in the grand expanse,
In the strings of essence, we partake the dance.

Architect of Reverie's Domain

In dreamscape's realm, the architect soars,
Foundations laid on subconscious shores.
Majestic spires of thought rise high,
Under the boundless, limitless sky.

Melding wishes with the stones of sleep,
The mason of mindscapes builds them deep.
Corridors twist and chambers align,
In the palace of slumber, all designs intertwine.

With visions drafted on the walls of rest,
Each dreamer a guest in the nest.
He crafts from the ether with tender care,
So each may dwell in a refuge fair.

The architect toils in the silence of dreams,
Where reality merges with fantasy streams.
Through his hands, he grants the keys,
To the wonderous sanctum of night's soft ease.

The Enigma of Inspiration's Sprout

In the mind's quiet garden hidden deep,
A seed of thought begins to gently creep.
It sprouts in silence, far from daylight's shout,
A mystery, where inspiration sprouts.

Beneath consciousness, it twines and it grows,
Eluding grasp as the subconscious flows.
It draws from the well of the unexpressed,
A tender shoot from inspiration's crest.

This sprout unfurls, its leaves touching the skies,
With hues unseen by any painter's eyes.
A bloom of notions in perpetual drought,
Inspiration's enigma sprouting out.

From fertile silence comes the artist's shout,
When inspiration's sprout has finally sprouted.

Whittling Wands of Wonder

With chips and shards, the shavings fall away,
Revealing stories locked in wood's array.
A carver's hands, with whispers soft and thunder,
Give shape to dreams in whittling wands of wonder.

Each stroke unveils a form from fantasies,
As curls of wood join with the drifting breeze.
The wand begins to hum, to sing, to ponder,
A conduit for spells it weaves and wanders.

The grain holds myths, a history untold,
In each whirl a magic that unfolds.
These whittled sticks ignite a child's blunder,
Becoming more, these wands of sheer wonder.

Enchanted by the lore within the wood,
We weave the world as only dreamers could.

An Architect's Dreamscape

On parchment plain, an architect's dream lies,
A conjured world beneath a draftsman's eyes.
With lines and curves, a symphony's scape,
In graphite shades, an escape takes shape.

Towers rise from realms of reverie,
Bridges arch over imagined sea.
Concrete and steel from paper leap,
In slumber's grasp, where designs sleep.

Blueprints bloom like gardens of stone,
From seeds of ideas that have been sown.
A city breathes in a sketch's sweep,
Cradled in an architect's deep keep.

Within this draftsman's dreams, they rise and dip,
Skylines born from the mind's tight grip.

The Mystic's Blueprint

In the silence where the cosmos twirl,
The mystic scribes a hidden swirl.
Symbols etched on ancient skin,
A blueprint of the light within.

Stars align on papyrus old,
Secrets in the stardust, bold.
The path is charted, quiet, and clear,
For those who seek to hold truth near.

Mysteries drawn in circles wide,
Within the mandalas, spirits hide.
Each line a whisper of the divine,
In the sacred text, they intertwine.

So gaze upon this cosmic chart,
And find the blueprint in your heart.

Illuminating the Unwritten

Words unspoken, dreams untold,
Paths unwalked, yet to unfold.
In the silence, thought takes flight,
A canvas bare, in need of light.

Two lines meet, a story's birth,
A pen ignites, gives dream its worth.
Shadows dance in the candle's hue,
Illuminating what we never knew.

Each line a journey through the night,
In the darkness, we find our sight.
Letters mingle, they twist and weave,
In the unwritten, we believe.

Words of wonder, without an end,
To the heart and soul, they tend.
Uncharted realms of the mind's own nation,
Herein lies true illumination.

The Origami of Existence

Fold by fold, life takes shape,
Intricate lines of a silent escape.
Each crease a memory, subtly ingrained,
An existence crafted, uniquely framed.

A corner bends, a new dimension,
A simple turn shifts our attention.
Life's origami, complex and plain,
Whispers tales in each vein.

From paper thin moments we arise,
Under the vast and endless skies.
Our edges sharpen, as years pass by,
In the origami of existence, we fly.

With gentle hands and tender care,
Shapes of hearts and souls we share.
The art of living, precise and true,
In each fold, a world anew.

The Forgotten Language of Creation

In the beginning, silence spoke,
A tongue of fire, a spiraling smoke.
A language lost in the sands of time,
Woven deep in the cosmic rhyme.

Ancient words on the breeze did dance,
Choreography of fate and chance.
Syllables sown in the stars' vast sea,
The lexicon of what was to be.

Within the earth, a whisper stirs,
The forgotten language that Time blurs.
Songs of the stones, rhythm of the rain,
In every echo, the old words remain.

We are the heirs to this primal speech,
In every wave, in the lessons they teach.
In hallowed whispers, the past we hear,
Creation sings for those who dare to revere.

The Tinker's Quiet Contemplation

Within walls lined with ticking thoughts,
The tinker toils, tying time in knots.
Cog upon cog, the rhythm of mind,
Seeking the answers that we hope to find.

Glimmers of insight in a gear's embrace,
Clockwork reflections of an earnest face.
Between each tick, a silent truth,
The journey of age, the zeal of youth.

With every turn, an idea's birth,
A small invention, a new-found worth.
The quiet hum of the brass abates,
As in contemplation, the tinker debates.

In this space where silence reigns,
Creativity flows through seasoned veins.
Through the hush, a world is spun,
In the tinker's gaze, all becomes one.

The Brewer's Secret Recipe

In the whispering vats, magic ferments,
A secret brew that time accentuates,
With hops and grains in perfect alignment,
A concoction that the palate celebrates.

Beneath the cellar's antiquated beams,
Lies the alchemist in his liquid dreams,
As yeast and brewer collaborate unseen,
Crafting the amber in clandestine streams.

Every bottle, a story untold,
Rich with tradition, and flavors bold.
A recipe guarded through the years,
A symphony of laughter, cheers, and cheers.

With every sip, a legacy flows,
An artful blend that only the brewer knows,
Hidden notes upon the tongue do dance,
In the spirited pirouette of serendipitous chance.

The Silent Drama of Design

Lines and curves in quiet discourse,
In the realm of the silent drama, a powerful force.
Silhouettes speak in the absence of sound,
Crafting illusions, ingeniously bound.

White spaces breathe in silent plays,
Embracing the void in a myriad of ways.
Contrast and balance wrestle in the mind,
In the canvas's duel, resolutions we find.

Beneath the surface simplicity lies,
A world of meaning in clever disguise.
Colors converse in the visual feast,
Whispers of style, from the greatest to least.

The silent drama commands its stage,
In fonts, in hues, in the golden age,
A dialogue mute, yet eloquently clear,
A timeless vernacular, the world holds dear.

The Enlightened Penman

In a well of ink, ideas begin to swim,
Words are the pawns, and thoughts the king.
The penman scribes, a dance of refined hand,
On parchment stage, the prose expands.

With each stroke, a picture is painted anew,
Of human follies, and truths construed.
The quill's journey, from chaos to art,
Transcribing the whispers of the enlightened heart.

Philosophy carved on the fiber of trees,
Narratives birthed with the greatest of ease.
The penman—the sage of the inscribed word,
In the flight of the script, the soul is heard.

Within the grip of an enlightened state,
The scribe begets worlds that forever resonate.
In ink drops, wisdom and fantasy blend,
A legacy scripted for generations to mend.

The Gardening of Myths

In the garden of legends, myths take root,
In the fertile soil of time's astute.
Stories flourish, a spectral bouquet,
Blossoms of lore that never decay.

Each seedling, a narrative sown with care,
Watered by fantasies spun from air.
Ageless tales sprout under celestial breaths,
Fed by the sun, untouched by deaths.

The garden keepers trim the epic fronds,
Where hero and beast form their timeless bonds.
In the hedge maze of the heroic jest,
Lie eternal quests put to the test.

Here in this horticultural realm,
Myths are tended, with fables at the helm,
In the gardening of the perennial script,
Enchantment blooms, in tradition dipped.

The Seamstress of Dreams

In twilight's hush, her needle threads,
Through weaves of starlight, silken spreads.
With tender stitch and gentle seam,
She sews the fabric of each dream.

The moon her lantern, soft and gleam,
Guides her hands in the flowing stream,
Of hopes and whispers, love's sweet tryst,
In each fold, a dreamer's wish.

The tapestry of night, so vast,
Holds her creations, made to last.
Each delicate snip and careful tie,
Brings to life dreams that never die.

A tapestry of slumber's lease,
Woven with threads of tranquil peace.
As dusk retreats and nightfall draws,
She crafts the dreams without a pause.

Conjuring the Silent Symphony

In the quietude where whispers dwell,
A baton rises, and with its swell,
Notes unplayed, start to assemble,
In a concert hall, silent, yet nimble.

A maestro of mute, guides the air,
With invisible notes that aren't quite there.
In silent waves, the melodies breathe,
An orchestra's hush, beneath the sheathe.

Each unheard sound, meticulously planned,
Floats through the vacuum, like grains of sand.
A masterpiece written in the void,
A symphony silent, but not devoid.

The audience, rapt in still attention,
Feels the music, a spectral invention.
In the soul, the quiet plays on,
Conjuring the silent symphony, now gone.

Potter's Wheel in Motion

Upon the wheel, the clay does spin,
A dance of fingers, thick and thin.
Round and round in rhythm's hold,
A formless lump takes shape, bold.

The potter's hands, firm yet kind,
Coaxing the earth, with the mind's design.
Every groove a whispered secret,
In the whirling mud, a silent sonnet.

Wet and smooth, the surface curves,
Under deft motion, it twists and swerves.
A vessel grows from the potter's dream,
In the dance of wheel, a steady beam.

Centrifugal force meets artistic will,
The wheel slows down, the air grows still.
A creation set from spin to stand,
The potter's wheel yields life to hand.

The Invisible Inkwell

In the shade of my mind lies an inkwell unseen,
With it, I paint thoughts, on a canvas serene.
Dipped in the silence, my quill starts to dance,
Drawing dreams out of air, given form by chance.

This ink from within, it flows without end,
Crafting verses unheard, on which souls can depend.
In the words that I write, the invisible shows,
A script of the heart, where the unseen prose grows.

A scribe of the night, where shadows hold sway,
My inkwell spills silence in a luminous way.
Each stroke is a whisper, each line is a thought,
A collection of musings, with memories fraught.

The reader's mind's eye can follow each trace,
Of the thoughts that were penned with invisible grace.
From my invisible inkwell tales do pour,
Leaving the reader to seek, to discover more.

Birthing the Boundless

Within the silent void it stirs,
A nascent cosmos softly whirs.
Infinite realms of space unfurled,
A newborn universe is twirled.

From chaos order finds its way,
As stars ignite to break the grey.
Galactic dance in endless night,
Each spiral arm a beacon bright.

Vast oceans of the dark expanse,
Swirling nebulas entrance.
From such abyss does life emerge,
Creation and the void converge.

Eternal cycles thus commence,
In the theater of existence dense.
With every birth and every loss,
The boundless weaves and spins its cross.

Fishing in the Stream of Consciousness

Beneath the surface thoughts do glide,
A silken stream, consciousness' tide.
With mental rod cast deep within,
I seek the musings to begin.

The shimmering ideas bite,
On hook of focus, held to light.
Reeling in the notions vast,
I capture fleeting thoughts that passed.

By water's edge of introspect,
I sort the catch that I collect.
Pondering the ones that shine,
In this secluded stream of mine.

Baited with the quiet mind,
The deepest insights I do find.
My introspective fishing trip,
Where wisdom in the ripples slip.

The Puppeteer's Intuition

With strings so fine, they braid the air,
The puppeteer with flair does dare.
Each subtle twitch and twist of wrist,
Great scenes of silent tales consist.

Intuition guides the dance,
Of marionettes in entranced trance.
Invisible to watching eyes,
His deft control, the heart's surprise.

Behind the scenes, the strings converge,
As characters with life emerge.
A symphony of motion weaved,
By hands unseen, the crowd's deceived.

And so he plays with fate and chance,
Each movement tied to hidden lance.
With strings of intuition spun,
The puppeteer and dolls are one.

Knotting Gossamer Thoughts

Within my mind, thoughts light as air,
A gossamer of strands so fair.
With nimble fingers, I entwine,
Ideas that lightly dance and shine.

I knot the wisps of fleeting dreams,
Their complex patterns glow and gleams.
A tapestry of mind's creation,
Woven with delicate concentration.

Thought threads that in the sunlight glow,
Each knotting brings a new tableau.
In silent contemplation's loom,
I craft the whispers of my room.

With every twist and careful plot,
New insights in the weave are caught.
From tangled threads, clear thoughts are sought,
In gossamer is wisdom brought.

The Invisible Tapestries

In whispers woven without a seam,
Across the silent loom of dreams.
Threads of thought, too faint to see,
Tangle in the mind's quiet streams.

Each strand a tale, a hidden plea,
Crafting visions we never speak.
An unseen art, where spirits free,
Dance upon the canvas bleak.

Ghosts of feeling, soft and flighty,
Patterns in the air, they leap.
Transcendent yarns craft stories nightly,
In the gallery of sleep.

The invisible tapestries hang uncaught,
In the alcoves of our sighs.
In every thread, a notion wrought,
With every knot, a secret lies.

Beneath the Artist's Veil

Behind the canvas, truths untold,
Where colors hide the artist's soul.
The strokes are bold, the hues are frail,
Veiling the tale that must unfold.

An intimate dance of shadow and light,
A silent symphony played on sight.
Pain and passion in disguise,
Unveil the soul that painting hides.

Each line a whisper from within,
Each hue a fragment of the mind.
The artist peers through life's thin skin,
Seeking the truths that lie behind.

Beneath the veil, a secret space,
A storied sanctum none perceives.
Herein lies the artist's grace,
The soul's mosaic one achieves.

Brushstrokes on the Spirit

A canvas bare, the soul awaits,
For colors to define its fate.
With every stroke, emotion states,
The depth of life we illustrate.

The palette holds a spectral range,
Of feelings deep and wisdom strange.
A masterpiece beyond exchange,
With every tint, the heart's exchange.

Upon the spirit, paint will dance,
A rich, resounding visual trance.
In every move, a new romance,
Where art and destiny advance.

The final work, both bright and cryptic,
Emotions etched in hues prolific.
The spirit's portrait, drawn unrestricted,
In strokes that speak the art terrific.

Weaving the Dream's Fabric

In the loom of night, the dreams commence,
With silken threads of subtle sense.
The spindle turns, the fibers tense,
Weaving the endless dream's incense.

A tapestry of sleep's own make,
Each pattern forms a story's take.
The colors blend for memory's sake,
In the quilt that souls will undertake.

Through warps and wefts of thoughts untold,
The dreamer's secret yarns unfold.
With every crossing, new worlds mold,
In the fabric, wonders are stowed.

Awake, the weaving seems surreal,
Yet in our hearts, the threads are real.
In dreaming, we begin to heal,
Under the loom's fantastic wheel.

Drafting Visions in the Dark

In ebony silence, sights unseen,
Crafting dreams where light has never been,
Gentle whispers in the void part,
Drawing futures with a shadow's art.

Blank canvas dressed in night's mystique,
Hands move in a language they speak,
Plotting stars in inky streams,
Tailoring the fabric of surreal dreams.

Lines emerge, they twist and twine,
Sketching thoughts from the divine,
Visions dance, they softly embark,
On cosmic journeys drafted in the dark.

Each stroke imbues a silent spark,
Where wonder wanders through the stark,
Here the night, in its grand arc,
Holds the pen that drafts visions in the dark.

The Lyricist’s Unspoken Verses

In quietude, the lyricist sighs,
A symphony in silence lies,
Notes hover in the space between,
A song unsung, unheard, unseen.

Words dangle from the poet's tongue,
A verse for every star unsung,
A rhythm felt but not played out,
Echoes within a silent shout.

In the heart where emotions swirl,
The lyricist's pen begins to twirl,
Crafting ballads without a sound,
In a world where their voice is bound.

Unspoken verses, tender, profound,
In the depths of the soul they're found,
To the surface, they rarely breach,
Yet in dreams, they sing and reach.

Birthing Galaxies Within

Within the mind's vast, boundless scape,
New universes take their shape,
Stars ignite from thoughts alight,
Birthing galaxies within the night.

Nebulae bloom, ideas entwine,
In the cosmic nursery of the mind,
Planets form of hope and fears,
Orbiting the sun of inner spheres.

Comets blaze in creative rush,
Leaving behind inspiration's flush,
Asteroid belts of fragmented lore,
Hold the stories yet to explore.

Dark matter binds the thoughts unseen,
Gravity of what could have been,
Each mind, a space of infinite spin,
Birthing galaxies deep within.

The Glassblower's Breath

With a breath, the art begins,
In furnace fires, the craftsperson grins,
A spherical dance of heat and glass,
A fragile future, shaped and cast.

In the glassblower's careful poise,
A spectrum caught in silent noise,
The molten sand, now liquid bright,
Reveals a world in translucent light.

Curved are the whispers of the breath,
Molding life from a tube of death,
Vases, sculptures rise with flair,
Air instilled by the blower's care.

As the glass cools, its fate is set,
Hardened tales of sweat and fret,
Each clear form, the breath's last trace,
The glassblower's gift to empty space.

Taming the Creative Kraken

In depths of mind where thoughts amass,
A kraken stirs, its tentacles entwine.
Ideas clash, and waves do crash,
Seeking structure in the brine.

Two lines away from chaos pure,
A sailor's hand must guide with lore.
With inky script, begin the lure,
Crafting order from the uproar.

Tales unfurl like sails in wind,
The monster's grasp becomes a pen.
From the abyss where dreams begin,
Emerges art from creature's den.

So I shall tame, with steady gaze,
The beast that in my psyche plays.
And navigate the mental haze,
To birth the kraken's vast displays.

Orchestrate the Sullen Muse

With baton poised and stage all set,
The sullen muse, she somberly waits.
Conductor's hands weave a silent net,
To capture song before it abates.

A harmony crafted from the mute,
A symphony born of silent strings.
Each note a phonon, without refute,
From dour silence, melody springs.

The podium holds a world's fuse,
Ignited by the quietest fire.
With mind as guide, none can confuse,
The muse no longer wrapped in mire.

Lift her veil, begin the dance,
Orchestrate where silence grew.
The quiet muse given her chance,
To grace the world with something new.

Knitting the Ethereal Quilt

With threads of starlight softly spun,
Knitting the quilt of the ethereal night.
Each stitch a tale, a moon, a sun,
Weaving dreams until morning light.

Celestial patterns in her hands,
Labors of love 'twixt warp and weft.
The tapestry of many lands,
The loom of time, her deft theft.

Beneath a canopy of sighs,
Cocooned in folds of nebulae.
Sleepers dream under her skies,
In the comfort of her worldly lay.

Knit one, purl two, the cosmos yields,
To the gentle pull of her cosmic strings.
In the silence, the universe reveals,
The quilt where eternity clings.

The Composer's Quill

With every stroke, the quill declares,
A note, a chord, a key, a time.
Composing scores on staff-lined wares,
Scribing symphonies sublime.

From silence sculpted, sounds emerge,
Quill dances, twirls, an artful siege.
The music's surge becomes a dirge,
Or lifts aloft in a joyful league.

The ink, the quill's immortal blood,
Flows flush across the paper's veins.
Bringing to life a tuneful flood,
Where each rest echoes and sustains.

A maestro with a feathered sword,
Cuts through the quiet air with skill.
The empty page now fully scored,
With notes that the composer's quill has spilled.

Weaving Thought's Fabric

In solitude's embrace, my thoughts take flight
Each stitch in time weaving black and white
Patterns emerge from the depths of night
A tapestry of ideas, glowing bright

The shuttle moves in silent reverie
Creating worlds only I can see
Thought and memory interlace, set free
In the loom of mind's vast tapestry

With every twist a new design found
A quiet insight, in silence profound
Dreams and reason intimately wound
In the fabric of thought, I am bound

This inner garment, uniquely mine
Threaded with strands of the heart's fine twine
It cloaks my soul in a design divine
Weaving thought's fabric, line by line

Painter's Vision Quest

A stroke of brush, a burst of hue
The artist's eye seeking something true
Landscapes drenched in morning dew
Panoramic vistas in view

Canvas speaking in silent cries
Colors blending like sunrise skies
In each pigment, a dream complies
A vision quest through painter's eyes

Through swishing sounds, the vision grows
Each azure sweep, a wind that blows
Upon the easel where magic flows
The painter's vision, finely composed

With every hue a world takes form
Beyond the norm, a haven warm
In painted dreams, emotions swarm
On this vision quest, my spirit's born

The Tapestry of Inner Echoes

Soft whispers dance in the corridors deep
Echoes of the heart that never sleep
Each resonance, a secret to keep
In the tapestry where memories weep

The needle pricks, as past times call
Stitching echoes in the hallways tall
With each echo, I recall
A life lived fully, echoes enthrall

A thread of joy, a shade of sorrow
Weaving the echoes of every 'morrow
The inner loom spins without borrow
Preserving today for the echo's morrow

So let these echoes form a design
A complex weave of yours and mine
A tapestry where our lives entwine
Inner echoes in time's confine

Alchemist's Dream Diary

In scrolls of old, where secrets lie
A tome of dreams under midnight sky
Alchemy's touch, in pages sly
A dream diary, where myths apply

Transforming lead to gold in dreams
Within the mind, where thought gleams
A philosopher's stone, or so it seems
In the alchemist's diary, ambition teems

Distilling hopes in a crucible's glow
Transmuting fears, letting go of woe
Elixirs of wisdom slowly grow
In dream diaries, the knowledge flow

Each page a universe to explore
Dreams alight, to the core
Riddles penned in ancient lore
An alchemist's dreams, forevermore

Illuminating the Secret Chamber

In whispers of the sable night, a glow,
Within the hushed and hidden room awakes.
The light, a soft and golden luster, breaks;
It bathes the chamber's secrets we must know.

A tale of times and treasures long ago,
Illuminated past a shadow's flakes.
Each corner, crevice, cranny light partakes,
Revealing what the dark refused to show.

A beam of knowledge shines on silent thoughts,
Touching ancient lore with tender care.
Resplendent rays on history alight,
And in their glow, understanding is sought.

The light, a truth-teller extraordinaire,
Gives the chamber's heart to the night.

Hands Dancing with Destiny

With fingers skimming over fate's vast loom,
The weaver's hands fly fast as lightning's flash.
In twists and turns, the threads of life they dash,
Entangling joys with sudden strokes of gloom.

They dance with purpose, spinning in the room,
Connecting moments with a delicate sash.
In the intricate web, dreams and hopes clash,
Interwoven in time's expansive womb.

Yet graceful still, amidst the tangled reels,
They sew the fabric of a tale complete.
A tapestry of destiny revealed,
With every choice and chance that they meet.

Hands cup the future, gently they can feel
The pulse of ages in their own heartbeat.

The Innate Architect

Within the mind's eye lies the blueprint clear,
An architect of innate craft and skill.
Transcending stone and steel with sheer will,
The dream's foundation sets without a fear.

Bricks laid in thoughts, so strong and yet so dear,
A vision's fortress, rising on a hill.
Each corridor and hall designed to fill,
With creativity that we revere.

This innate force that shapes the silent clay,
With every curve and arch, it tells a tale.
The structures, in their standing, seem to say:
In mind's own mansion, creativity's the sail.

Unseen yet felt in what we do and play,
The architect's own world, where thought prevails.

Etching the Emotional Landscape

Beneath the tranquil surface waters lie,
Emotions' hues that paint the heart's terrain.
They ebb and flow like currents of the brain,
An endless sea beneath the psyche's sky.

A joyous peak where golden sunbeams fly,
A sorrow's trench where tears fall down like rain.
This landscape bears the bliss and bears the pain,
In the silent depths where feelings vie.

Through rolling hills of passion and of plea,
The ridges carved by laughter and by cries.
In every ridge and hill, the truths we see,
Etched deep within the essence of our eyes.

The canvas of the soul, vast, unconfined,
Mirrors the emotional landscape of the mind.

Chiseling the Silent Voice

In the quiet, a whisper grows,
A silent voice that no one knows,
Chiseling through the still night air,
Dreams take shape from what's not there.

With every stroke, the voice takes form,
A soft, ethereal being born,
From marble of the muted breaths,
Life emerges, defying deaths.

The voiceless words now resonate,
Carving out a silent state,
Echoes of the unsaid thought,
In sculpted silence, speech is wrought.

And there it stands, a figure clear,
A silent voice we all can hear,
It speaks in shadows, dances light,
Chiseled whispers housed in night.

The Loom of Thoughts

Weaving through the mind's great loom,
A tapestry of blossomed bloom,
Sharp colors of the thoughts we weave,
The patterns only we perceive.

Threads intertwine, ideas clash,
A vibrant, ever-changing sash,
Each strand a memory unforgot,
A piece of mind’s convoluted plot.

The shuttle flies, the fabric grows,
With every thought the texture shows,
A canvas of the heart and brain,
Where joy and sorrow leave their stain.

And when the last thread finds its place,
We'll step back to admire the space,
For in the loom of thoughts, we find,
The woven essence of the mind.

Molding the Ethereal

With hands of hope we wish to mold,
The ethereal into our hold,
A shapeless mass before us lies,
Beneath the vast, unending skies.

We press and push with tender care,
To give it form, refined and rare,
With every touch, a purpose found,
In the silence, a whispered sound.

The air itself lends breath to life,
Molding peace from out the strife,
A transient beauty, here and made,
In ethereal light and shade.

Though time will claim our crafted feat,
Its fleeting dance is no less sweet,
For in the mold of air and dream,
We capture life's ephemeral stream.

Sculpting the Mind's Clay

Sculpting the clay within our skull,
The potter's wheel spins full and dull,
Ideas rise with every turn,
In the kiln of thoughts they burn.

Gentle hands of mind at play,
Shaping the cerebral clay,
Creating folds of intellect,
A masterpiece we self-reflect.

Fingers trace the curves of will,
Crafting grooves of skill with skill,
Within the mind's uncharted maze,
Our inner substance finds its ways.

The final piece is never done,
Under the ever-changing sun,
For moldable is the mind’s grey clay,
Transformed with each and every day.

Whispering Hands of Creation

In silence, the universe speaks, serene,
With hands that whisper life into green,
The artist's breath, a gentle inflow,
Casting worlds in a soft-glowing sheen.

Stars, like fingertips, dance and weave,
Tracing the vault of night, they conceive,
A tapestry vast, in cosmic loom,
Where dreams are born, to stay or to leave.

Rivers of time carve valleys anew,
Pondering the old, embracing the true,
Nature hums with creative light,
In every hue, a world-view to construe.

Mountains rise with stories untold,
Unseen hands sculpt the earth's bold fold,
Creation’s symphony, a hushed sound,
Crafting beauty that never grows old.

In the Atelier of the Soul

Behind the veil where thoughts entwine,
The painter dips in pools of brine,
In the atelier of the soul's own plight,
Each stroke of brush dictates the spine.

With colours mixed in pain and glee,
The canvas breathes life's decree,
In shades and hues that speak to none,
But to the heart, they whisper free.

Each layer a secret, veiled and keen,
Where tears and laughter are seldom seen,
The soul's raw essence captured fair,
In strokes of destiny, ever so lean.

The masterpiece of life, unique,
Within the atelier, softly speaks,
Of silent battles, won and lost,
On canvas where the spirit seeks.

Threads of Inspiration

A glimmer in the mind's eye caught,
Silken threads of inspiration wrought,
Weaving ideas from the air,
In every fiber, a story sought.

A loom of dreams in endless spin,
Crafting visions from within,
The warp and weft of hope entwined,
A fabric made of what might have been.

Across the quiet, an artist's hand,
Moves with purpose, bold and grand,
Tying knots of endless tales,
In every loop, a future planned.

With the final thread in place,
A tapestry of time and space,
A narrative rich, in vibrant mirth,
Unveiled for the world to embrace.

The Artisan's Heartbeat

In the rhythm of the hammer's dance,
A pulse that flows as chisels prance,
The artisan's heartbeat, steady and true,
Crafting passion with every glance.

Beneath the skin of oak and stone,
The sculptor carves his thoughts alone,
In every chip, a part of soul,
Embedded deep, to the marrow bone.

Fingers touch the grain with care,
As whispers of wood fill the air,
The heartbeat syncs with nature's call,
In a love affair beyond compare.

A final touch, the work complete,
The heartbeat slows, yet feels replete,
For in the craft, the life does beat,
An artisan's love, forever sweet.

The Aesthetic Alchemy

In whispers of the rustling leaves,
Beneath the sky's vast, endless dome,
Transmutes the leaden world we grieve,
To golden thoughts, our mental home.

A brush that paints not just a scene,
But souls of colors, pure, intense,
It crafts from mundane, the serene,
This alchemy of the sixth sense.

With every stroke, the canvas breathes,
The painter's eye casts spells unseen,
The tapestry of wonder weaves,
In threads of crimson, gold, and green.

For art is magic, subtle, grand,
A world within the world we know,
The work of an unseen hand,
That shapes the beauty from shadow.

The Engraver's Hidden Script

Etched upon the heartwood's grain,
A story waits in silence, deep,
The carver's hands, they craft the refrain,
Of mysteries the timbers keep.

In every curve, a secret lies,
A language only few can speak,
It whispers to the discerning eyes,
And echoes through the valleys bleak.

The engraver's blade, a silent poet,
Does dance upon the surface bare,
Inscribed, the hidden script does glow it,
A script that time cannot impair.

For in the wood the tales persist,
Of loves and losses, eternally scribed,
The carver's touch, like a tender kiss,
Through the hidden script, we're all described.

Murmurs of the Unpainted Brush

A canvas blank, a silent plea,
Whispers of bristles yet to dance,
In the theater of the unfilled sea,
Begging for that creative chance.

It murmurs dreams in hushed tones low,
Of colors bursting forth in joy,
A masterpiece in embryo,
Awaiting strokes that will deploy.

A brush that hums with patient wait,
To sweep across the virgin white,
It yearns to seal a vivid fate,
And fill the void with visions bright.

In unseen hues, it softly cries,
Invoking shades that soon will blend,
Upon the canvas, life defies,
The quiet, in a painted end.

Behind the Veil of Ingenuity

Behind the veil, ideas weave,
A dance of neurons, quick and slick,
The tapestry that minds conceive,
Is spun from threads both thin and thick.

In shadows of the mundane sight,
Lies brilliance veiled, awaiting flight,
Whose wings will spread in purest light,
And soar above on art's great height.

The Inventor's mind—a secret space,
Where miracles are dressed in thought,
Each notion has its given place,
In the gallery of the wrought.

Behind the scenes, the cogs align,
The blueprint of the new unfurls,
Within the genius, divine,
Lies the power that changes worlds.

Stitches in the Cosmic Fabric

Whispers of cosmos, silken threads intertwine,
Galactic tapestries, the celestial design.
Needles of starlight, piercing the dark veil,
Sewing constellations, a shimmering trail.

Unseen hands weaving through time and space,
Connecting the dots in an endless embrace.
Patterned skies tell an ancient story,
In the fabric of universe, we glimpse glory.

Each stitch a moment, a heartbeat of stars,
Quilted in quiet by the moon and by Mars.
The fabric enfolds every dream ever spun,
In the cosmic expanse, we are all as one.

Seeding Thought's Blooming Garden

In the garden of the mind where ideas take root,
Thoughts blossom like flowers, wisdom the fruit.
Seeds scattered by wind, by chance or by will,
Sprouting in silence, in stillness, they fill.

Nurtured by curiosity, watered by dreams,
Under the sun's knowledge, each petal gleams.
Thickets of notions, some wild, some refined,
In thought's rich soil, endless mysteries unwind.

Each seedling a question, greeting the sky,
Vines of reflection, ever aiming high.
Bearing the harvest of enlightenment yearned,
The garden thrives, as the seasons turn.

In the Studio of Solace

In the quiet studio where solace paints alone,
The canvas listens gently, to every sigh and moan.
With brushes dipped in the pigment of the heart,
Each stroke a refuge, a silent work of art.

The colors mix in whispers, in shades of peace and woe,
Solace finds her texture in the ebb and flow.
A gallery of comfort, for eyes that seek to rest,
In the studio of solace, the soul is gently blessed.

There, every masterpiece is born from gentle hands,
Pain and joy commingle, like distant, tender lands.
The easel holds the memories, each one softly drawn,
In the studio of solace, our deepest selves reborn.

Sketching the Unseen Horizon

A pencil traces the line where dreams and daylight meet,
Scribing unseen horizons, where earth and sky greet.
The artist’s hand moves in concert with aspiration's guide,
Outlining futures hidden, where hope and truth reside.

In the quiet hush before dawn, the sketch begins to bloom,
Drawing out the promise of light from the gloom.
Horizons yet to be seen, born from shades and line,
Hold the artist's vision of a world redefined.

Canvas of possibility joins in the dance of creation,
Embracing each pencil mark, it fuels imagination.
There, the unseen horizon, where tomorrow’s sun will
rise,
Is etched with the hope of dawn, beneath the infinite skies.

The Alchemy of Imagination

In the cauldron of the mind, ideas brew,
Whispers of color in the world's hue.
Alchemist's visions that dance and sway,
Transmute the night into gold kissed day.

A tapestry woven with dreams so bold,
In the secret loom where tales unfold.
Reality's fabric, in fancied flames,
Imagination's power never tames.

Elixir of wonder, in thought's realm found,
Where possibility knows no bound.
Crafting new worlds from the ether's womb,
Life painted afresh in imagination's room.

From mere thought to creation's grand door,
Dreams alchemize into myths of yore.
In minds deep, such magic is spun,
The endless alchemy, never done.

Echoes from the Inner Workshop

Within the silent workshop of the soul,
Echoes resonate, completing the whole.
Hammers of heartbeats, chisels of thought,
Crafting the self, tirelessly wrought.

The artist within, silent and wise,
Listens to whispers that never dies.
Each echo a lesson, a memory's spark,
Lighting the caverns that lie in the dark.

The inner echo, a symphony played,
On instruments of spirit, skillfully made.
In every pulse, a story's rhythm,
A journey through the self's deep chasm.

This workshop's echoes, our guiding voice,
Help us to make each crucial choice.
In silent musings, we find our way,
Echoes leading to a brighter day.

Carving Our Essence

With every moment, chisel in hand,
We carve our essence, grain by strand.
Life's block of marble, rough and wild,
In our own image, tenderly styled.

Through trials we sculpt, with love and pain,
A figure emerges through the strain.
Each chip falls away, a story's part,
Revealing the sculpture that is our heart.

Our essence is shaped, day by day,
By choices we make, by work and play.
Underneath the stone, what will we find?
The truest reflection of heart and mind.

Carving our essence, a lifetime's art,
Mindful strokes from the very start.
In the sculpture of self, the truth is key,
Carving our essence, we set it free.

The Silent Symphony of Being

In stillness lies a silent symphony,
A composition of being, vast and free.
Notes in the air, unheard but felt,
In the quietude where presence dwelt.

Beneath the bustle, a steady hum,
The rhythm of life, to which we succumb.
Each breath a beat, each heartbeat a chord,
In the silence, our peace is stored.

Through unspoken music, we understand,
The harmony held in life's quiet hand.
Vibrations of existence, soft and clear,
A symphony inside that's always near.

In the hush, the universe resonates,
A concert of cosmos that contemplates.
In being's silence, we find our tune,
Under the quiet sky and the silent moon.

Silhouetting the Intangible

In shadows cast by mind's own light,
Betwixt the grasp of day and night,
Silent echoes fill the air,
Woven threads of thoughts so rare.

Silent muses dance in gleam,
Spinning webs of half-dreamt dream,
Contours vague in twilight's hug,
Ideas on perception's rug.

Fleeting whispers, soft and vague,
Formless tales that thoughts beguage,
Silhouettes of musings bend,
In the mind's eye, without end.

Cast upon the canvas mind,
Forms of the unformed kind,
Intangible, they evade our clasp,
Yet in their mystery, we gasp.

Embered Thoughts Aflame

A spark ignites in the silent dark,
A fire born from an inner mark,
Embered thoughts begin to flame,
In the hearth of soul, they claim their name.

Each flicker burns with a secret word,
Stories unheard but inwardly stirred,
Rising smoke of the lost and yearned,
The pages of mind are softly turned.

In the heat, memories gently char,
Glows undimmed by life's bizarre,
Ashen dreams drift to the sky,
As hope kindles, too wild to die.

Aflame within, this hidden art,
Keeps warm the caverns of the heart,
Though fires dwindle into embered glow,
Their heat remains in the afterglow.

Ode to the Unheard Symphony

In the quietude of an unseen stage,
Orchestra tunes of an unwritten page,
Strings vibrate in silent harmony,
Playing an unheard symphony.

Breezes hum with the trees' soft sway,
Nature conducts in a grand ballet,
Dewdrops chime in morning's glee,
Each a note in this wordless spree.

Whispers of life in the rushing brook,
A melody forgotten, no place in a book,
Rustled leaves in a symphonic rush,
Compose the ballad in the twilight hush.

Our senses seek the subtle song,
That the universe plays all lifelong,
An ode to the symphony never heard,
Yet felt in the heart, deeply stirred.

Smithing the Phantom Forge

In the anvil of thought, the hammer swings,
Shaping phantoms into invisible things,
Forging dreams with the mind's great force,
Smithing ideas on a spectral course.

Sparks fly from the phantom forge,
Where imagination and reality merge,
Glowing concepts are bent and twined,
In the smithy of the artist's mind.

Heat of passion, bellows breath,
Crafting visions, defeating death,
Metal spectres in the air do swirl,
The hammer shapes a hidden world.

With each strike, a purpose melds,
In the smithy where the spirit dwells,
Forging onwards, through the fantastic door,
Where thoughts become the phantom's core.

The Woodworker's Whisper

In the forest's hush, beneath the sentinel trees,
The woodworker listens, a whisper in the breeze.
With hands that dance, and eyes that keenly glean,
He shapes silent tales in every grain unseen.

Two shavings curl, like ribbons cast aside,
A testament to skill, where precision and art collide.
The scent of pine and sawdust fills the air,
While chisels craft dreams with tender, loving care.

The mallet tap-taps, a soft, rhythmic hymn,
Each stroke brings life from the wood's quiet whim.
Burled patterns emerge, the natural maze unfurled,
A wooden tapestry from the heartbeat of the world.

Then comes the final piece, with care imbued,
A creation not just made, but lovingly wooed.
Within its fibers, a whisper can be heard,
Of the woodworker's passion, in every crafted word.

Dancing with Invisible Ink

Her pen glides across the paper's silent stage,
Dancing with ink that's clear as the morning's first light.
Words pirouette, unseen actors out of their cage,
In a ballet of thoughts that twirl far from our sight.

Through the waltz of emotion, her heart seeps,
Invisible ink, the dance of feelings deep.
With each blank page, a promise to keep,
The canvas awaits the dreams that leap.

Moonlight's embrace unveils the secret dance,
Revealing the words, as if by chance.
They shimmer and shine, in night's romance,
A silent sonnet, an ephemeral glance.

When the dawn returns to claim the sky,
Her whispered verses, in sunlight, will lie.
Though once hidden, now they boldly fly,
Invisible no more, their truth never shy.

Forging Imagination’s Alloy

In the foundry of thought, where ideas are wrought,
The blacksmith imagination stokes flames of lot.
He folds and he hammers, on the anvil of dreams,
Blending visions and memories in passionate schemes.

Sparks leap and they dance, as metals combine,
Fusing wonder with reality in a design so fine.
Tales of gold, and silver threads of lore,
The alloy takes shape, stronger than before.

Molten concepts pour into molds of hope,
Solidifying aspirations on a vast kaleidoscopic scope.
A sculpture of fantastical hues and might,
Unveiled in the gallery of the mind's own light.

With each strike, a new world begins to form,
From the fiery furnace, ideas are born.
Imagination's alloy, both malleable and strong,
A testament to creativity, where all dreams belong.

The Luthier's Silent Song

The luthier works in a room of quiet tones,
Crafting harmonies in wood and strings alone.
Each stroke of his plane, a note in the air,
Fashioning an instrument with the utmost care.

In the curls of the shavings, a melody hides,
Waiting to emerge as beauty abides.
Fingers trace contours where music will linger,
Drawing out songs with the touch of a finger.

Strings are laced and tensioned with grace,
Each twang a whisper in the silent space.
He hones and adjusts with an ear finely tuned,
Anticipating the ballads that will be crooned.

In the final embrace, the silence is broken,
A luthier's silent song, a symphony unspoken.
The instrument sings with each bow and pluck,
A crafted echo of life, from hands that struck.

Whispers of the Artisan Soul

In the hush of dawn's soft light,
The world feels pure and new,
The artisan's soul whispers bright,
In strokes of crimson hue.

Gentle hands craft love’s own form,
Between earth and sky they toil,
Creating beauty, warm and warm,
From the soil, air, and turmoil.

Each hammer's fall, each chisel's kiss,
On wood or stone, in focused trance,
Whispers of truth, in silent bliss,
Where hands and heart advance.

In the echoes of the empty space,
Resides the soul's own plea,
Crafting legacy with grace,

For all the world to see.

Symphony of Silent Inspirations

Through the din of life, hear the quiet call,
Melodies of thought, where silent inspirations fall,
Notes that hover in the air, unseen symphony,
Catching them in minds, where they're meant to be.

In the heart of night, whispers rise and soar,
A ballet of ideas, each one yearning for more,
They waltz around the soul, in a quiet dance,
Every silent inspiration, a serendipitous chance.

The mind conducts, with a baton unseen,
Harmony from quietness, a leap so keen,
A crescendo of notions, without a sound,
Invisible orchestra, inspiration profound.

The symphony plays, though never heard,
Silent inspirations, by inner muse stirred,
In the quiet, a masterpiece begins to form,

A testament to silence, where ideas swarm.

Heartstrings of Imagination

On the canvas of the mind, images swirl,
Heartstrings plucked by thoughts that twirl,
Imagination's dance, a hidden delight,
Painting desires in colors so bright.

Dreams weave through the pattern of stars,
Chasing the sun, and Venus and Mars,
Orbiting in the vast black, the mind's great sea,
In the heart’s secret depths, what will you see?

Each pluck of the string, a story starts,
Crafting worlds, in the gallery of hearts,
Tales spun from whispers, and the echoes within,
Adventures that beckon, let the journey begin.

In the quiet, listen to the heart’s sweet rhyme,
Where every beat’s a verse from an untold time,
With every pulse, the imagination takes flight,

Boundless, brilliant, in the heart’s own light.

Plying the Threads of Creativity

Fingers dance upon the threads of thought,
Weaving tapestries from what the world has taught,
In the loom of the mind, ideas interlace,
Spinning the yarns that time cannot erase.

Colors blend, from the spectrum of dream,
In the fabric of creation, a shimmering seam,
Patterns emerge, bold and unconfined,
In the textured cloth of the weaver's mind.

Stretching fibers, twisted and entwined,
With each knot tied, a new concept is defined,
Textures of joy, shades of sorrow's weave,
Plying the threads that our stories conceive.

In endless creation, hands never tire,
Through the warp and weft, passion's fire,
And thus we create, from morning until eve,

The infinite possibilities that we believe.

Printed in the USA
CPSIA information can be obtained
at www.ICGtesting.com
LVHW010525171223
766606LV00005B/178

9 789916 395196